Published 1987
by Merehurst Press
5, Great James Street
London WC1N 3DA
by arrangement with
Temps de Pose Editions
12, rue de Sévigné
75004 PARIS
TELEX 215313 F

© 1987 Editions Temps de Pose
Photos copyright © 1987 : Pierre TOUTAIN
Text copyright © 1987 : Gilles MERMET
ISBN 0-948075-69-4

Layout : Corinne REYMOND
Photocomposition : Graphelec, Paris and Scheuble & Baumgartner, Berlin
Printed in Italy by SAGDOS-Brugherio-Milano
Translated by Veronica HAMMOND

TIBET

Photographs
Pierre TOUTAIN

Text
Gilles MERMET

MEREHURST PRESS
LONDON

The kingdom of pure waters

*The Yamdrok Tso lake is located at 5,000 m above sea level.
It is the domain of Lu, the water spirit.*

Juniper for the gods

A family of pilgrims offer smoke to the spirits.

The wife of a warrior

The khampas mountain people remain unconquered by the Chinese; the open smile belies the impenetrable face of Tibet

Resistance

"I am sorry, Sir, I don't speak Chinese!"

Tenzipalgor, the tiny shaven-headed monk dressed in a worn woollen robe, was being bombarded with questions by the green-capped regiment surrounding him: the ten officers of the Chinese People's Army seemed capable of swallowing him alive! But Tenzipalgor held his own confidently, in spite of his pint-pot size:

— "I must repeat," he said "that I cannot speak Chinese. I can only speak Tibetan and a few words of English."

The atmosphere was tense, aggravated by my attentive presence and my complicity with the child-monk. We were in the Dalai Lama's private apartments at the peak of the Potala mountain, one of the most visited and also one of the holiest places in Tibet, a few feet away from heaven ...

How would the Chinese extricate themselves from this linguistic muddle? The green-capped heads bent in discussion. The senior officer finally turned to the monk and explained, no longer in Chinese, but, bowing to the inevitable, in English, "We have lost our way. You must show us the way out." Tenzipalgor acquiesced. As they plunged into the dark maze of corridors the officers smiled self-consciously and saluted me with inscrutably Oriental face-saving politeness.

An everyday scene? No, a scene which epitomized the Tibetan imbroglio. Han Chinese soldiers on a "mission" to Tibet, lost in the Dalai Lama's palace (how symbolic!), asking a "fellow-countryman" the way in the language of "Western imperialism" — a comic Chinese puzzle.

Tenzipalgor reappeared, grave-faced. For him it was a typical Sunday, bringing tourists and groups of Chinese soldiers to visit the Potala, the fortress of a once glorious country; an ordinary Sunday in the life of an occupied, afflicted country without a future. Tenzipalgor crouches in the evening sunlight and takes up the mournful chanting of his mantras.

Witnessing this scene I realized that when I entered Tibet I had plunged into a tragedy; that I had set foot on a maimed land of glory and that, from then on, pathos would be inherent in everything I saw, touched and felt.

As a backdrop, there was a vast setting the size of western Europe, an immense plateau hauled 13,000 feet (4000 metres) into the air by awe-inspiring forces. The most direful catastrophe of the planet gave birth to this fateful land! Fifty million years ago India collided with Asia and plunged under and into it, raising Tibet as if with a wedge.

Buddhism forbids sadness.

Even today the Himalayan giants continue to grow — under the earth crust of the high plateaus, angry demons roar perpetually! Sometimes the earth quakes and splits apart, revealing its bowels through gaping disfiguring cracks; or the seismic vibrations push rocks and hills heavenwards!

Tibet offers neither sweet prettiness nor serene valleys: it is a land reduced to essentials, on which temperate joys cannot survive. Peace and luxury are to be found in another world: a world reserved for the meritorious, after cycles of searching and suffering... At this height the superfluous has disappeared. In order to resist the onslaughts of wind, cold, dust and the burning rays of the sun, nature in her infinite diversity has eliminated the most fragile creatures and only kept the toughest: fungus, barley, goats, sheep, yaks and man.

Here geology and geophysics, tectonics, paleomagnetism and seismology combine to study the folds, the cracks and the vibrations of the human soul. In the icy solitude of Lake Nam Tso a thousand years of imitation have turned the nomad's face into a landscape, a blistered earth-crust with its cracks, its dried-up river beds and its great turquoise-blue salt lakes ...

Here, in close proximity to heaven, the Tibetans invented God, and in

Burning juniper and incense in prayer.

order to ward off evil spirits from the underworld became shamans priests or seers. The Bonreligion was born. Human sacrifices were offered to the spirits of the mountains and the wells and to the protectors of the tents.

During the sixth century AD the love of a king and the charm of a king's wives introduced Buddhism into Tibet: the king was Songtsen Gampo and his pious and beautiful wives were Brituki Devi from Nepal and Wen Cheng Konjo from China. Thus began the extraordinary story of a people whom nature had isolated from the rest of the world and whose greatest achievements were to become purely spiritual and intellectual. Temples and monasteries sprang up all over the country and grew into large centres of teaching and worship, the pillars of faith in a better world: man's pathetic response to his harsh antagonistic surroundings, which he could at last rise above.

Tibet as a whole was to organize a hierarchical society around one spiritual principle which was at the same time a political virtue: the quest for wisdom and happiness through the relinquishment of material values. At the peak of the hierarchy sat the Dalai Lama who was the spiritual and temporal ruler of the Tibetan people: the "Living God" who was always the reincarnation of his predecessor. When a Dalai Lama died, the lamas consulted oracles and with the help of esoteric signs "discovered" in a child prodigy the new incarnation of their ruler. This extraordinary spiritual electoral system, introduced in the fourteenth century by the Gelukpa Buddhist order of monks the famous "Yellow Hats", has allowed a succession of Dalai Lamas to remain in power until the twentieth century!

The second degree of the Tibetan hierarchy comprised a circle of "Living Buddhas" revered as great lamas and abbots who were also incarnations of their predecessors. They dispensed their excellent teaching to a mass of monks and novices, who might be sons of peasants or of lords, whose sole ambition was to become lamas in their turn.

But to attain the paths of wisdom the novice had to respect more than three hundred monastic rules, to lose himself in meditation, to do penance and to show himself an apt pupil in the study of Buddhist writings, philosophy, logic, rhetoric and metaphysics. Otherwise his spiritual career would stop short in the kitchen, the workroom or the vegetable garden! Whether one was a lama or a lay brother, what mattered most was to serve one's country spiritually to the best of one's abilities. Until 1950 one third of the male population was in holy orders; the smallest village had its monastery or its hermitage.

In that theocratic state there were also some lay figures of whom the most powerful were the great lords who divided their time between the care of their estates and the affairs of the State. All political and administrative appointments were held by a nobleman in tandem with a churchman. Thus laymen and monks supervised one another to prevent corruption...

The peasants owed their lives and their work to the local lord and throughout their miserable existences had to provide the monasteries with gifts in kind: cattle, grain, butter and cheese, which might help them to achieve a more fortunate reincarnation in their next lives. If he could not pay his taxes, the unfortunate peasant could appeal to his fellow-serfs for help, but if this failed, he would become a beggar or a slave. In that arduous life, religion, not revolution, was the panacea. Tibet never experienced a peasant revolt in fourteen centuries. Before 1950 a man was born a serf or a nobleman and the only way to rise in the social scale was to enter a monastery: a situation which gave rise to no complaints. Did that mean that the peasants' lives were not unenviable? According to Buddhist belief, their present suffering resulted from sinful actions committed in a previous existence... and only by offerings and prayers could they hope for a happier future life. On the high plateaus our lofty conception of happiness has no place.

Cut off from the world, these "visionaries of God" lived in a closed universe where comparisons were impossible, a universe in which liberty could only be gained through the salvation of the soul and in which the only equality was that of prayer.

That is Tibet, the forbidden land that Alexandra David–Neel, the woman with "winged heels", discovered at the beginning of the century. A country that had banned all foreigners but an untouched country which was to fascinate her all her life, a fascination her readers were to share...

That is Tibet as it was, timeless, hammering out eternity to the sound of the trumpet and the beat of the drum during festivals, rhythmically marking out the year from the songs of the sowing to the dances of the harvest —

free to live its life and its faith in the vertigo of its terrible immensity and head-reeling heights!

That was Tibet ... up to the day when horror submerged the country!

When the iron bird takes wing and horses gallop on wheels, Tibetans will be scattered world-wide and Dharma will leave for the land of the Red Man.

The Indian seer Padmasambhava wrote this fearful prophecy in the eighth century. Today it is engraved in blood-red letters on the minds of all Tibetans.

On October 26, 1950, in the first glimmerings of dawn, Tibet was brutally hurtled into the twentieth century, petrified like a man condemned to death: Mao Tse-tung's troops had invaded the eastern province of Kham. They swept aside the intrepid Khampa warriors who were armed with sabres and obsolete guns! The Dalai Lama appealed to the United Nations. Fruitlessly. Tibet was already nothing more than a legend ...

A few months later, the Chinese entered Lhasa. A peaceful force. Their aim? "To free Tibetans from the forces of imperialism" (what "forces of imperialism"?); "to take Tibet back into the embrace of the mother-country" (Tibet had never been part of China); "to bring progress and economic development" (Tibet lacked roads, electricity and piped water and hardly knew the wheel had been invented — progress was something it could very well do without!) Brute force imposed its law ...

The first years of Chinese occupation were relatively mild, because the Chinese interfered only discreetly: building a few roads, schools and hospitals and so hoping to seduce the Tibetan people with technical innovations into "following the shining path that leads to socialism." But the people were indifferent. Their "shining path" led elsewhere...

So the Chinese interference became more ruthless. The Tibetan resistance took shape around the Three Pillars of the State, the monasteries of Drepung, Sera and Ganden. What could be done to convince this archaic society of the "advantages of the communist way of life"? There was only one way, the most radical and also the most Chinese: religion, the root of all evil, had to be extirpated.

And terror held sway over Tibet.

The first monasteries to be sacked were in the rebellious province of Kham; monks, yoked together and whipped forward, replaced yaks as beasts of burden. Mass executions took place. Nobles were buried alive up to the neck, then beheaded. Lamas were crucified or hanged with a heavy statue of Buddha as a counterweight. Cruelty became madness: to exterminate that rebellious people many Tibetan men were sterilised ...

Lhasa was on the verge of revolt. Its citizens thronged round the summer palace of Norbu Lingka to prevent the Dalai Lama from obeying a summons to China which had every appearance of being a warrant for his arrest. For the Lord of Tibet there was but one solution: exile. On March 18, 1959, the "Living God" left the capital for India.

"Tcharsawa!" (I will come back!).

He was never to set foot in Tibet again.

From then on, Tibetans were alone. Lhasa was put to fire and sword. Jokhang, the cathedral of Tibetan Buddhism and the heart of the resistance movement was bombarded; the Faculty of Traditional Medicine was razed to the ground; the chief monasteries were dismantled. The insurrection was crushed after three days of fighting.

*Many monks are
also craftsmen,
they maintain the monastery
and provide a
source of income.*

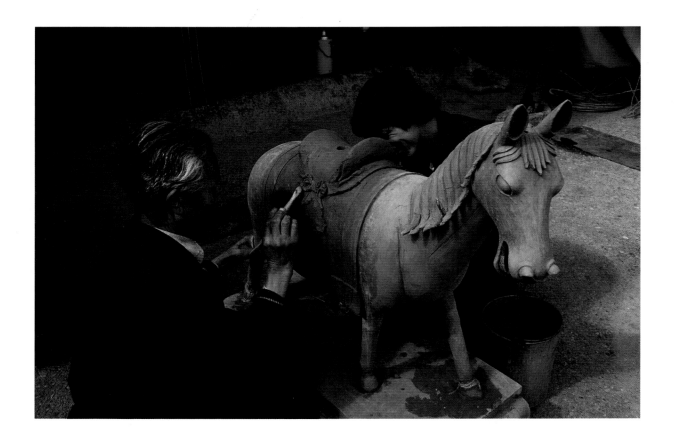

From then on, praying became a capital offence. Tibetans were forced to be present at show trials followed by public executions, which the families of the "guilty" had to applaud under threat of suffering the same fate. Indoctrination, imprisonment, torture, deportation, mass killings ... the Chinese used any and every means to reduce the Tibetans to submission. The more fortunate, a hundred thousand or more, fled this hell for India, Nepal, Sikkim or Bhutan. The Tibetan diaspora had begun.

For those who stayed, the apocalypse continued. In the 1960s the Chinese Cultural Revolution led to destruction of more than 2,500 monasteries which were sacked, then burned down or blown up by hordes of Red Guards who left not one stone standing in their frenzy. In the span of a few months Mao's China had destroyed the memory of an ancient civilisation. Only the Potala and a handful of monasteries were saved from the Red Guards' destructive rage. Aeroplanes were sent to bomb out the resistance groups in the mountains. Lacking organisation and allies, cold-shouldered by neighbouring countries, the resistance movement was to be routed and destroyed too. From then on Tibet was crushed under the heel of the Chinese while the unconcerned world looked on. The Tibetan night was to last for thirty years.

Today a new dawn glows on the horizon. A pathetic bitter dawn that is the aftermath of long dark nightmares. In 1979 the new regime in Peking brought a harvest of reforms to Tibet. The Chinese admitted their past errors: popular communes were suppressed; land and cattle were given back to starving peasants; winter wheat (a Chinese food) was replaced by the traditional barley; taxes were abolished; free markets, shops and tourism were encouraged.

And even more surprisingly, religion could be practised once again! There was an immediate and unexpected mass reaction: Tibetans brought out the buried statues of Buddha, Vajrapani, Tara and Mahakali: gods and saints hidden in the depths of the hearts and minds of a people — enduring and unforgotten.

Prayer wheels, beads, holy books, tangkas and mandalas were taken from their dusty hiding places; prayer flags fluttered once again in the Tibetan wind ...

The monks and lamas (or those who were left), who had been peasants for twenty years, threw away their Mao caps and boiler suits and put on monastic robes. Women displayed amber, turquoise and coral jewels; the Khampa horsemen plaited their hair with red braid. Tradition blossomed anew on every head and in every heart. Pilgrims from the farthest corners of the country hastened towards the holy shrines: in their place they discovered ruins ... or Chinese barracks!

The first prayers and the first offerings in a more clement atmosphere surprised the Chinese. Jokhang cathedral in Lhasa was overrun by Tibetan pilgrims! Thousands of people, a human anthill of ragged worshippers, were prostrating themselves or tirelessly milling round a temple open to the skies. The Chinese were taken unawares by such fervent piety. In Tibet for more than twenty years, the communist steamroller had destroyed everything, except the indestructible: religious faith!

Appearances had to be saved in the face of such a fiasco and the Chinese are masters in the art of masking reality. A subtle strategy was adopted: a certain freedom was conceded in the hope that no one would realise that it was totally illusory! Just a little whiff of liberty to assuage the yearning for independence. Once the wings had been clipped the bird could be freed from its cage ... The hypocrisy was obvious and no one was taken in.

Of course the Dalai Lama, after twenty years in exile, was invited back to his "mother country". Which "mother country"? Tibet? No, China! The "Living God" was to be transformed into a puppet and established in Peking from which he would be allowed to undertake very infrequent "inspection tours" in Lhasa — that is what the Chinese wished, since it would legitimise the integration of Tibet into China. The government in exile at Dharamsala in Northern India would lose all its moral authority over its people, who today more than ever look to the Dalai Lama for guidance.

The Dalai Lama has always refused to return under these conditions and his people are grateful. Obviously Tibetans hope he will come back but they know that he remains, secure on the other slope of the Himalayas, and will ever remain the sole undisputed ruler of Tibet, the incarnation of eternal Tibet, the guardian of its memory and its integrity.

The moral resistance of the Dalai Lama, supported by all Tibetans, keeps alive and strong the faith in a better future, however far away; a new age in which Tibet would live again, its liberty and independence achieved not by force of arms but by patience and persuasion.

Tenzin Gyatso, the present and fourteenth Dalai Lama said, "However strongly the wind of evil blows, it can never extinguish the flame of hope".

It is undeniable that religious centres are functioning again, but it is difficult to become a monk. The Chinese Bureau of Religious Affairs, a state department, controls all religious activities in Tibet. It winnows out then selects novices for the monasteries. Each monastery is directed by a "democratic commission" often headed by a defrocked lama. It goes without saying that before tasting the rare joy of Buddhist meditation and disputing in logic and philosophy, the candidate must acknowledge the "benefits of socialism". If the novice is a child his family must answer for him. If the Tibetan refugees exiled in Nepal are to be believed, the great restored Tibetan monasteries contain large numbers of spurious monks, actors in a gigantic masquerade who return to civilian life after their day's work. Tourists must have value for their money ...

Rumours are doubtless exaggerated ... but it is true that many monks show more zeal in demanding money when you take out your camera than in sharing the divine grace of their knowledge with you!

However, an attractive surface Buddhism has been carefully set out. It is true that a vast restoration campaign, financed by Peking, has been launched and that 200 of the 2,500 temples and monasteries that existed in Tibet before the Chinese occupation have been partly rebuilt.

Staunching past wounds was worthwhile if it made Tibetans swallow the bitter pill of the new reforms and if it attracted tourists, but how can monasteries, particularly Ganden perched on a 16,000 feet (5,000 metres) promontory and now a pathetic shell of half-demolished walls and foundations, recover their former splendour? The idea is totally illusory.

Of course progress has come: roads have been built, hospitals, dispensaries and schools have been opened ... Nowadays endless military convoys travel up and down, controlling the frontiers ... The drop in the infant mortality rate has filled the gap caused by the mass killings ... Education is making generations of children Chinese and imposing peacefully a new system of values ... Peking spends billions to maintain its authority and to administer the country but has never given Tibet the slightest genuine responsibility.

Who will gain from patient endurance: the Chinese or the Tibetans? The former, convinced that they have historic rights over Tibet will never give the country back its independence. Tibet, with its exceptional strategic value and its limitless mineral and energy reserves, has become part of China for good. It is now called the Autonomous Region of Tibet. Words, words, words...

Well then, what hope is there for Tibet?

On my way north on the road to Amdo where the Dalai Lama was born, I met a Khampa peasant ploughing his fields behind his sturdy yaks, black-haired dolmens with red plumes. I turned aside to greet him and held out a photo of the Dalai Lama. He stared at it, big tears rolling down his cheeks of wind, earth and sun. As a token of blessing he put the holy picture to his forehead, "The time will come... the time will come..."

He took up his plough again. Behind him his son was sowing the seeds of hope.

Glorifying the gods

Tibetan opera, its stories tell of the triumph of good over evil.

Thantog Gyalpo was
a great mystic.
He is credited with creating
Tibetan opera some 500 years ago.

*Opera is an offering
to the earth spirit...*

*... It is a joyous outpouring
of ritualistic dance, dialogue and music.*

A glimpse behind the mysticism

The child dreams
in the wings of the pageant.

27

*Opera provides an
opportunity for Tibetan
women to express
their femininity.*

In the mountains
the men and the yaks
share the load.

The ferryman work the icy meltwaters.

Piety at dawn.

*Prayer-flags are
hoisted to the gods.*

When the snows melt,
the Brahmapoutra river brings
life as well as disaster.

Horses and men

Harvest on the roof of the world.

Slaves to the land,
and ruled by the Chinese,
the Tibetans live a life governed
by the passing of the seasons.

The shepherds

*The Tibetans,
unlike the Chinese,
are allowed to have
large families.*

*The children,
hope for the future.*

A travelling people

A fire made at each stop is essential to the nomadic existence.

Human transhumance

All Asia moves together.

Lhasa is the centre of religious life in Tibet.

*Pilgrims travel for months
to visit Lhasa and seek the paths
to Buddhist wisdom and enlightenment.*

Tea is popular throughout Asia.

*A game of cards and
a hot yak-butter tea
provide a welcome break.*

Ancestral gaity...
... tasks that have been carried
out for a thousand years.

A doubly derisory world.
The sloth of the occupier...

... against the rock-like occupied.

A sunday picnic
is a family occasion.

The Chinese, like all occupiers,
bring along the materials
of seduction in their load.
Photography is now popular.

The charms of a child

The cheerfulness
of the conqueror.

In march 1959 Mao's China
crushed Tibet
in a bloody invasion.
The deep spiritual convictions
of the Tibetans remain
intact and prevent
them from becoming collaborators.

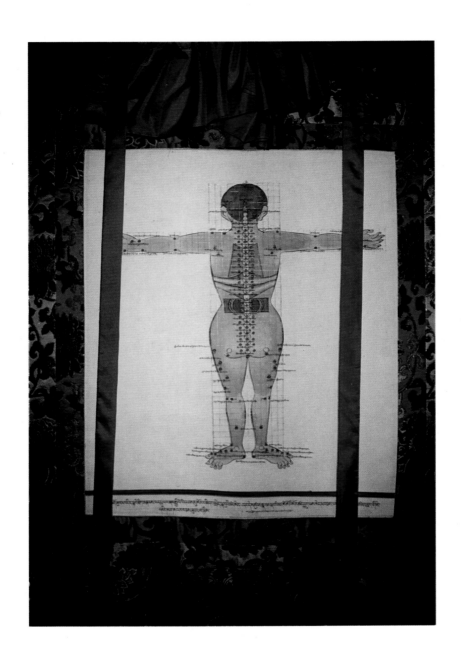

*The stange meeting
of art and medicine,
these tankhas provide
a visual record of
the secrets of Tibetan
healing methods.*

*Tibetan medicine is unique,
based on physical
and spiritual balances
of body and mind.*

The medical tankhas are used for reference,
all medicines are based on plants.

The Tibetan household, tenderness, and peaceful introversion are still a way of showing resistance to the Chinese presence.

*The contrasts of expressionism
a world away from Berlin.*

The Chinese prohibited
the use of the Tibetan language,
but have failed to assassinate
the ancient culture.
Today's children still learn
the language of their
ancestors.

The arduous road to knowledge.

The equation of internal freedom:
religion, trade and culture.

Rocks and boulders are painted with images of the dieties. They are considered to be holy places used for ritualistic and private devotion.

The Buddhist Agora

Jokhang palace is the meeting point of spiritualism and daily life...

Life is a circle of gold

The Jokhang is the central focus of religious life in Lhasa. The golden wheel symbolizes the buddhist vision of the unity of all things.

Worshipping Siddhartha.

*Many pilgrims prostrate
themselves at Barkhor.*

Buddha culminates here

The Potala palace, the centre of Buddhism in Lhasa.

*The disciples
read and re-read
the verses of wisdom.*

The buddhist faith is passed on from generation to generation. It is taught to the very young and does not discriminate between adolescence and adulthood. Faith culminates in old age.

The monasteries are run
on autarchical lines.
The monks have survived
because the only resistance
they have offered their
totalitarian rulers is that of
self-sufficient passivity.

The dialectic Sherpas

During the oratory contests gesture and speech are inveighed against each other.

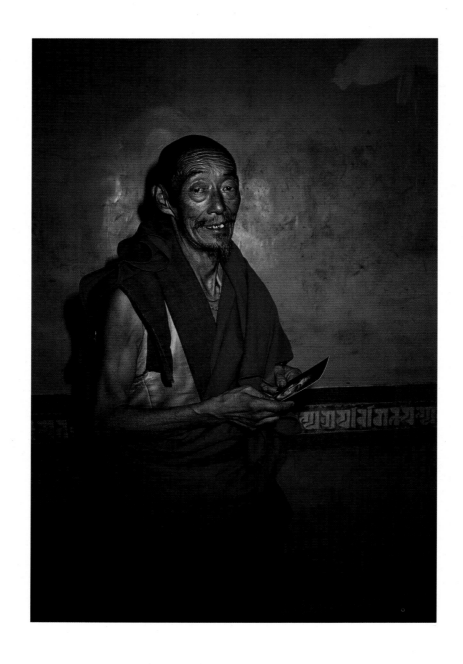

It takes between
twenty and thirty years
to become a monk.
Between twenty and thirty years
to learn the mantras by heart.
Between twenty and thirty years
to learn wisdom.

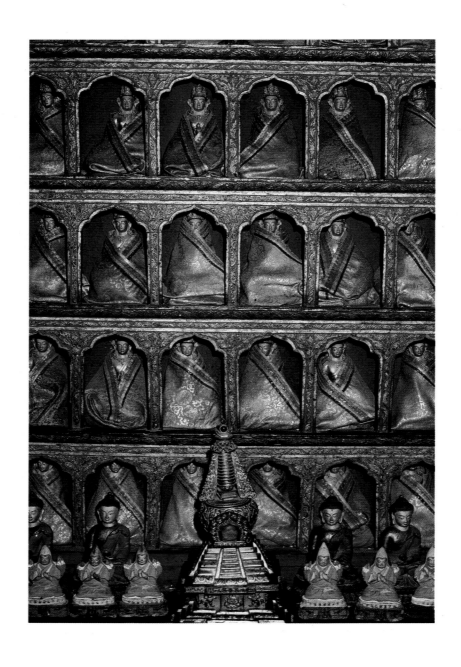

*The prayer-wheel
can contain millions
of prayers that are offered
to the heavens as they spin.*

The guardians of Buddhism.
The pilgrims place themselves
under their protection.

The eternal light

*Night does not exist
for the ever-watchful Buddha.*

Buddhism is a religion of many gods and dieties.

The lamps are fed by yak's butter.
Like the teachings of Buddha
the light is meant to be eternal.

*The XIVth Dalai Lama in exile in Dharamsala
expresses the true wisdom of Tibet.
He has written, "most of our suffering springs from
our impassioned desires and our attachment
to things that we falsely believe are
essential and durable".*

Interview with
his holiness the DALAI LAMA

Pierre TOUTAIN : First I would like to thank you for seeing us. The impression I have after spending one month in Tibet is that the Chinese have done a lot in Tibet : roads, offices, airports for their own use. In contrast to that I have visited some villages and I noticed that nothing has been done : no schools and in some cases no electricity. There is a very big difference between the Chinese way of living and the Tibetans'. After seeing all this, it seems very difficult, almost impossible, for you to go back to Tibet.

His Holiness the DALAI LAMA : There is no point in returning. We have a direct contact with the Chinese government. They pretend there is no problem in Tibet, and that the Tibetans are very happy. Only one thing bothers them : the Dalai Lama is outside the country. They have made some suggestions that I return, but my return is not important. What is important are the six million people living there. If they are really happy, if they have freedom or let's say free speech, if they accept voluntarily this situation, then one hundred thousand Tibetans will eventually go back, including myself.

At the moment the Chinese ignore the basic problem. There is no point in returning ; here I remain a free spokesman for the Tibetans. Although we are in a difficult situation, yet we have the Truth. We fight only for our own rights. We shall remain outside Tibet. The young people who have a political conscience prefer that I remain outside Tibet ; they do not want me to be a puppet in Chinese hands, although they are very eager to see me back.

Pierre TOUTAIN : I met some young Tibetans who told me that their parents have been very patient with the Chinese. They now want to fight and begin a guerilla war against the Chinese army ; could you tell me if this type of reaction is new in Tibet ? I know that of course you do not agree with violence, but do you think there is a

new generation coming with fresh ideas about how to obtain freedom ?

H.H. the DALAI LAMA : Yes, it seems that the young people want to follow a violent way. They want to carry weapons and fight. They take the Afghan guerillas and the Palestinians as their examples. I believe that this is impractical. Sometimes they criticize me, saying I am too soft.

Pierre TOUTAIN : They may, perhaps, say that you are too soft, but they do have such a strong respect for you. Nowhere in the world have I seen such devotion and love after twenty-eight years of exile : you are still the heart of Tibet. They are dismissive of the Panchen Lama (the most important religious leader left in Tibet). They claim that he is only a puppet in Chinese's hands. What do you believe ?

H.H. the DALAI LAMA: Deep down the Panchen Lama still believes and remains a freedom fighter under a rigidly controlled state of totalitarianism. He is compelled to say certain things which are against his own desires and his own wishes. When the Panchen Lama emphasizes that Tibet even in the past was part of China, he speaks under Chinese pressure.

Pierre TOUTAIN : You must have some news about the reconstruction of some temples. Do you know if there are serious plans to rebuild them ?

H.H. the DALAI LAMA : Many places are being restored. The local Chinese authority finally accepts that all this work must be carried out. They need to show a good image to the outside world and now to the tourists who visit Tibet. In some cases, they are giving money towards the rebuilding of the temples, but mainly it is taken care of by the local people. As far as I know the

The Dalai Lama,
the Living God,
is elected by the wise men
of Lhasa.

majority of these temples are used as museums. No one lives in them, there are no religious studies nor any serious religious practices. So you see the Chinese only allow people to walk around these buildings. There is no opportunity to study or to preach. Buddhism remains like a blank faith without knowledge. The religious freedom is very superficial but still may deceive. Even the former American President Jimmy Carter said last week that he was pleased by the religious freedom in Tibet.

Pierre TOUTAIN : As there is no possibility of studying to become a monk in Tibet, can you send some qualified lamas as instructors from Dharamsala back to Tibet ?

H.H. the DALAI LAMA : No. We cannot send monks. The Chinese would think that in the name of religion, the Dalai Lama is sending them for political

activities. It is impossible and useless. In the last few years, many young Tibetans who want to become monks and study have had no alternative but to escape to India. So far about one thousand young monks have come here : they pursue their studies in Tibetan monasteries among the Tibetan refugee community. For the preservation of Tibetan culture, Tibetan Buddhism, there must be a very intensive and deep study of religion. In order to become, a real Buddhist student, it takes twenty to thirty years of study. Nevertheless, there are around five thousand monks in India.

Pierre TOUTAIN : Have you, your Holiness, a message to our readers ?

H.H. the DALAI LAMA : You should tell the world that the Chinese presence in Tibet is colonial : the Chinese are committing a demographic genocide.

Despite being exiled,
the Dalai Lama remains
the spiritual leader of Tibet.

The power of Buddha is such that he is neither a prisoner of frontiers nor of violent ideologies.
The Tibetan refugees have taken their serenity with them.
These two lamas are now exiles in Nepal.

The eternity of the Buddhist faith
can be seen in the eyes of
these young monks.

*The life of Buddha is
taught trough frescoes.*

Temps de Pose Editions would particularly like to thank the following :